How Is a Crayon Made?

by Grace Hansen

abdopublishing.com

Published by Abdo Kids, a division of ABDO, P.O. Box 398166, Minneapolis, Minnesota 55439.

Printed in China

052017

092017

Photo Credits: Caters News Agency, Getty Images, iStock, Shutterstock

Production Contributors: Teddy Borth, Jennie Forsberg, Grace Hansen

Design Contributors: Dorothy Toth, Laura Mitchell

Publisher's Cataloging in Publication Data

Names: Hansen, Grace, author.

Title: How is a crayon made? / by Grace Hansen.

Description: Minneapolis, Minnesota : Abdo Kids, 2018 | Series: How is it made? | Includes bibliographical references and index.

Identifiers: LCCN 2016962385 | ISBN 9781532100437 (lib. bdg.) | ISBN 9781532101120 (ebook) | ISBN 9781532101670 (Read-to-me ebook)

Subjects: LCSH: Crayons--Juvenile literature. | Parafin wax--Juvenile literature.

Classification: DDC 688--dc23

LC record available at http://lccn.loc.gov/2016962385

Table of Contents

Making Crayons

Wax is delivered to crayon factories. At Crayola, railcars deliver the wax. The railcars are filled with **steam** to melt the wax.

The melted wax moves into large silos. Then it is pumped through pipes into kettles.

6
5
4
3
2

A few **chemicals** are added to the kettles. These chemicals will keep wax from sticking to the **molds**. They will also help make the crayons stronger.

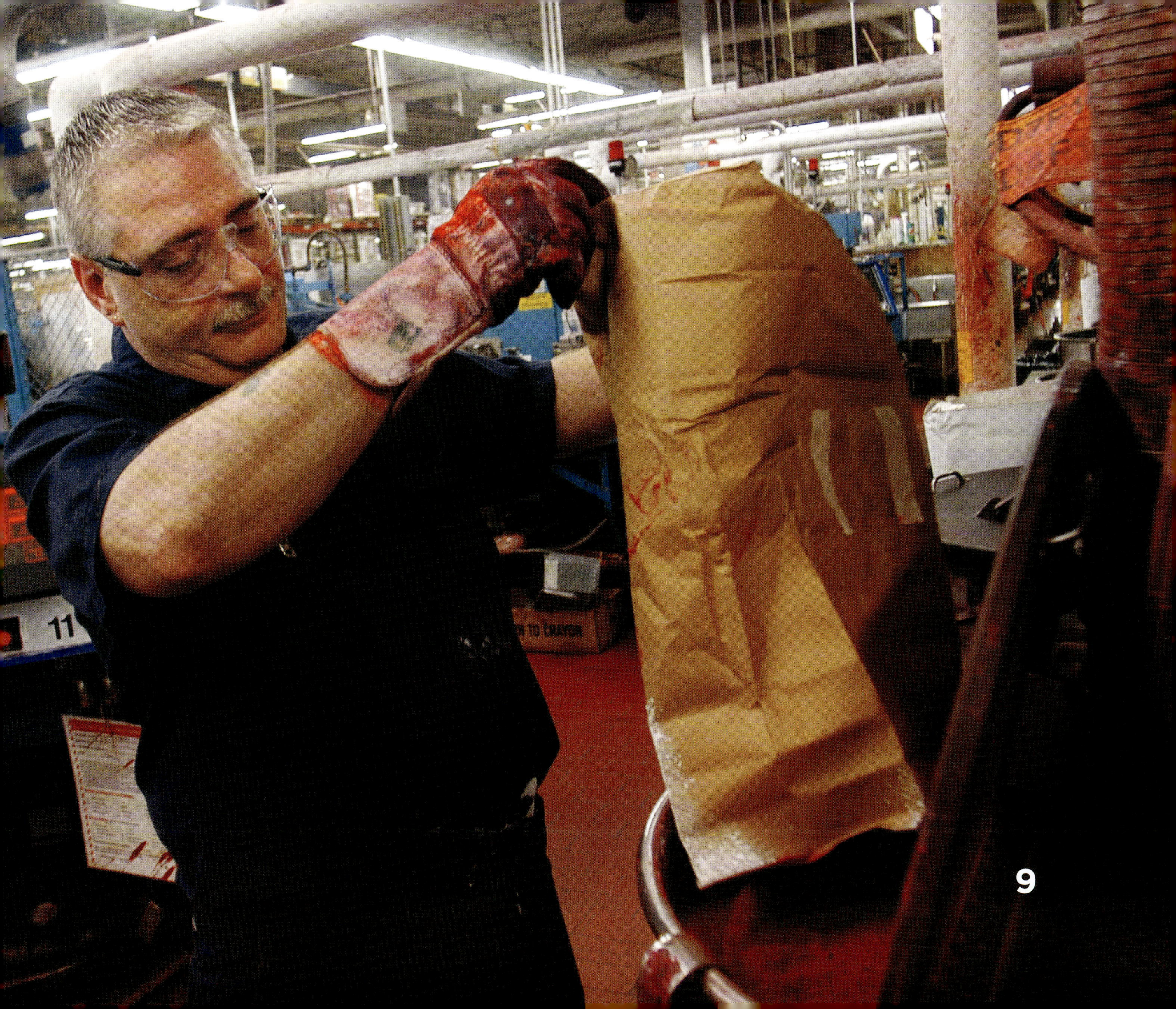
11
N TO CRAYON

Powdered color is added to the kettle. Everything is mixed together.

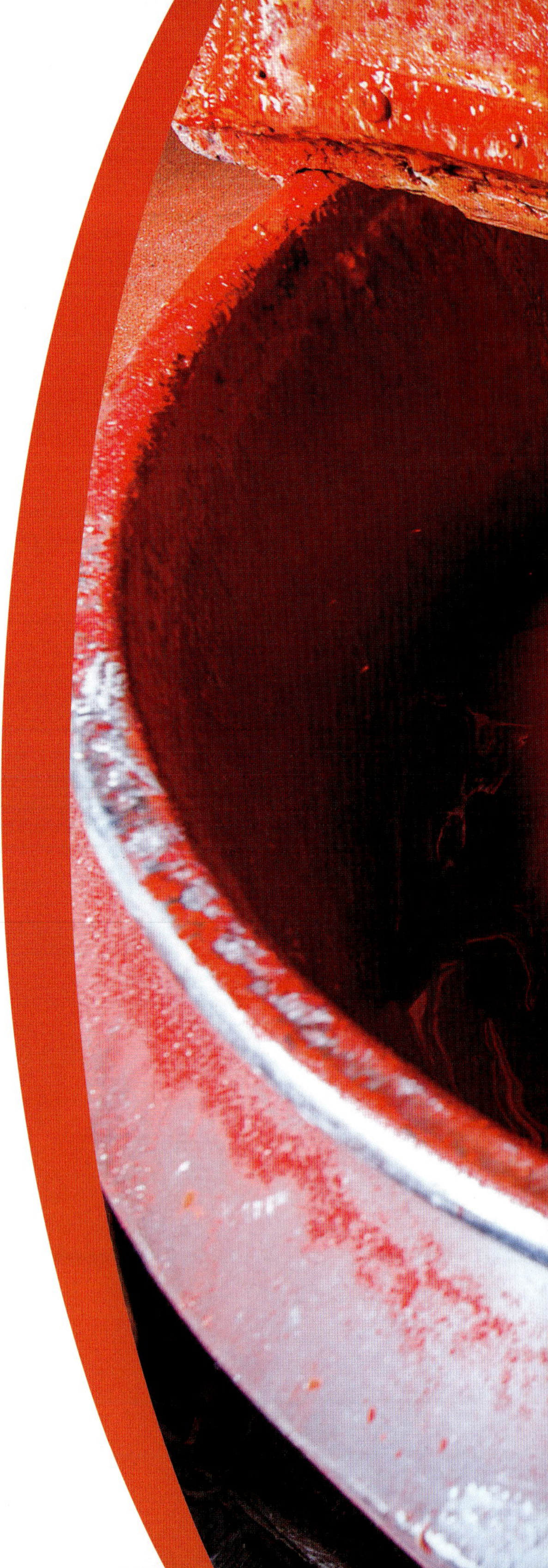

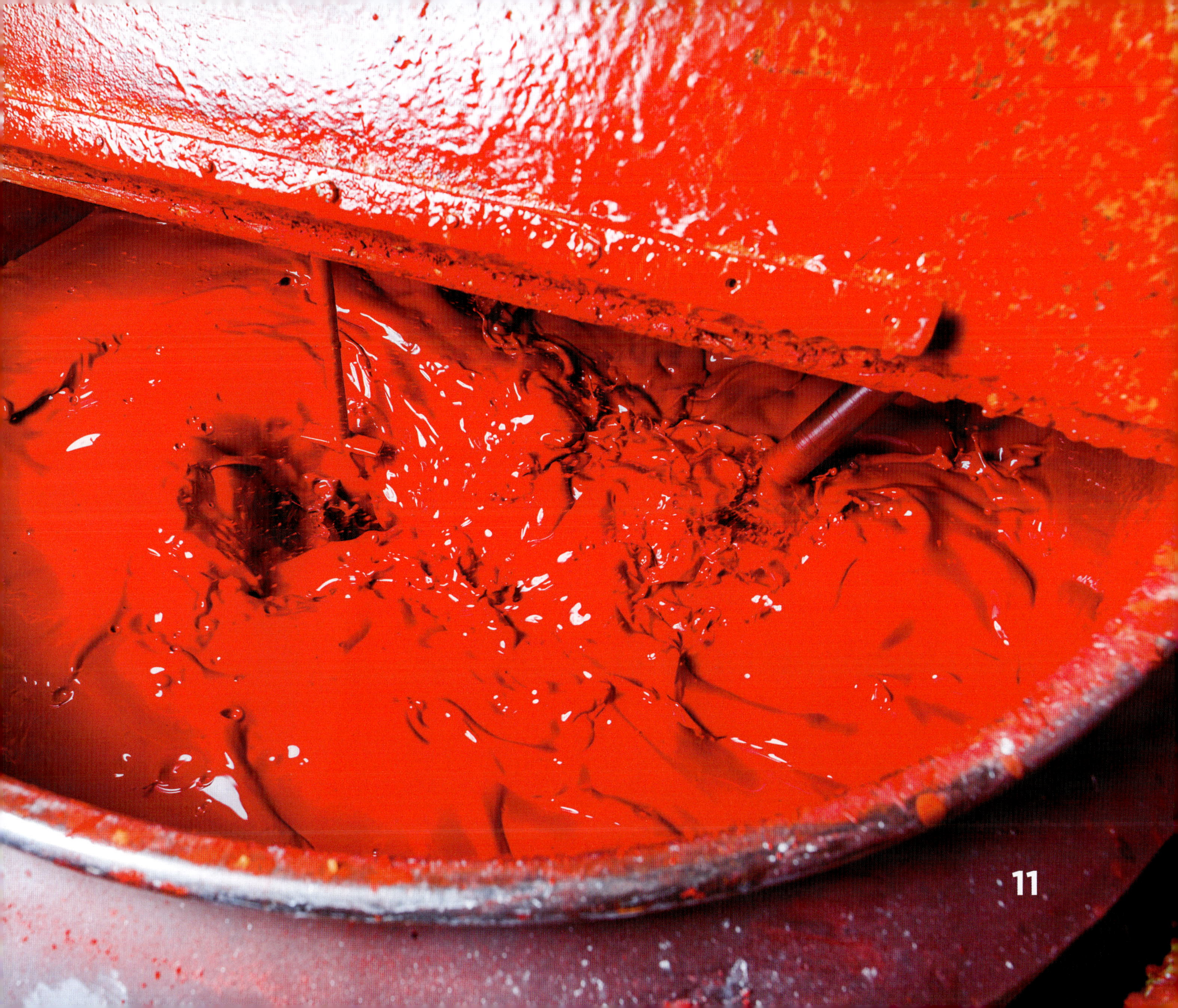

The newly colored wax is poured into **molds**. The molds are shaped like crayons. Everything is cooled and hardened with water.

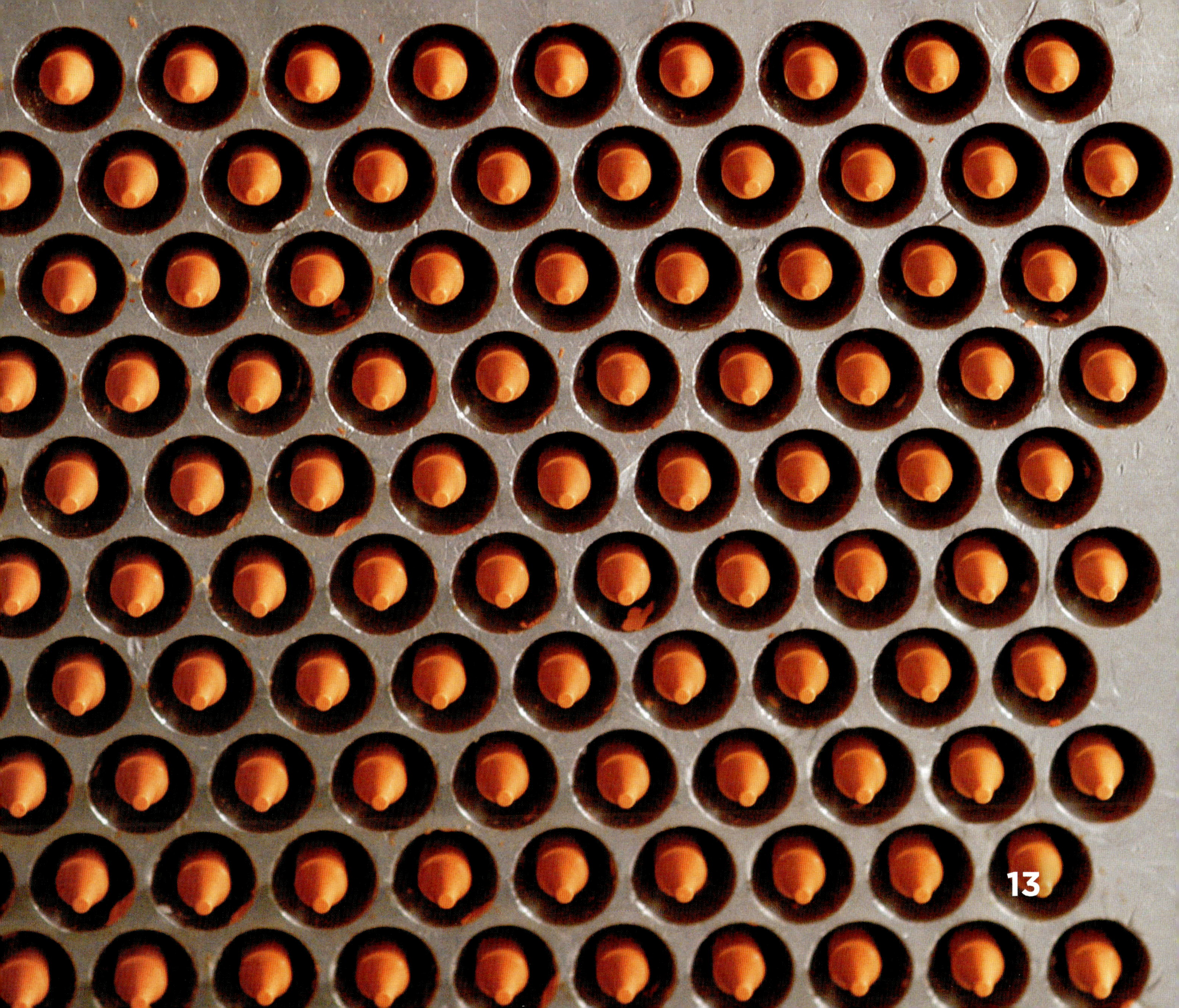

The crayons are pushed out of the **molds**. They are ready for labeling!

Crayola
Crayola.com

After they are labeled, the crayons move into containers. They are stored by color.

Crayola
CHALK
Crayola
So Big
Crayola

The crayons are dropped one by one. They **funnel** onto a platform. The crayons are swept into a box.

The Final Product

The boxes are sealed and ready for delivery! They are sent to stores around the world.

More Facts

- The largest crayon in the world is named Big Blue. It weighs 1,500 pounds (680.4 kg) and is 15 feet (4.6 m) long!
- Crayola, a crayon company, creates nearly 3 billion crayons a year.
- On average, a ten-year-old child has used 730 crayons in their life.

Glossary

chemical – a substance that has been created for a practical use.

funnel – to pass through a small opening.

mold – a hollow form that is meant to give shape to something.

steam – an invisible vapor that is created from boiling water.

Index

abdokids.com

Use this code to log on to abdokids.com and access crafts, games, videos and more!